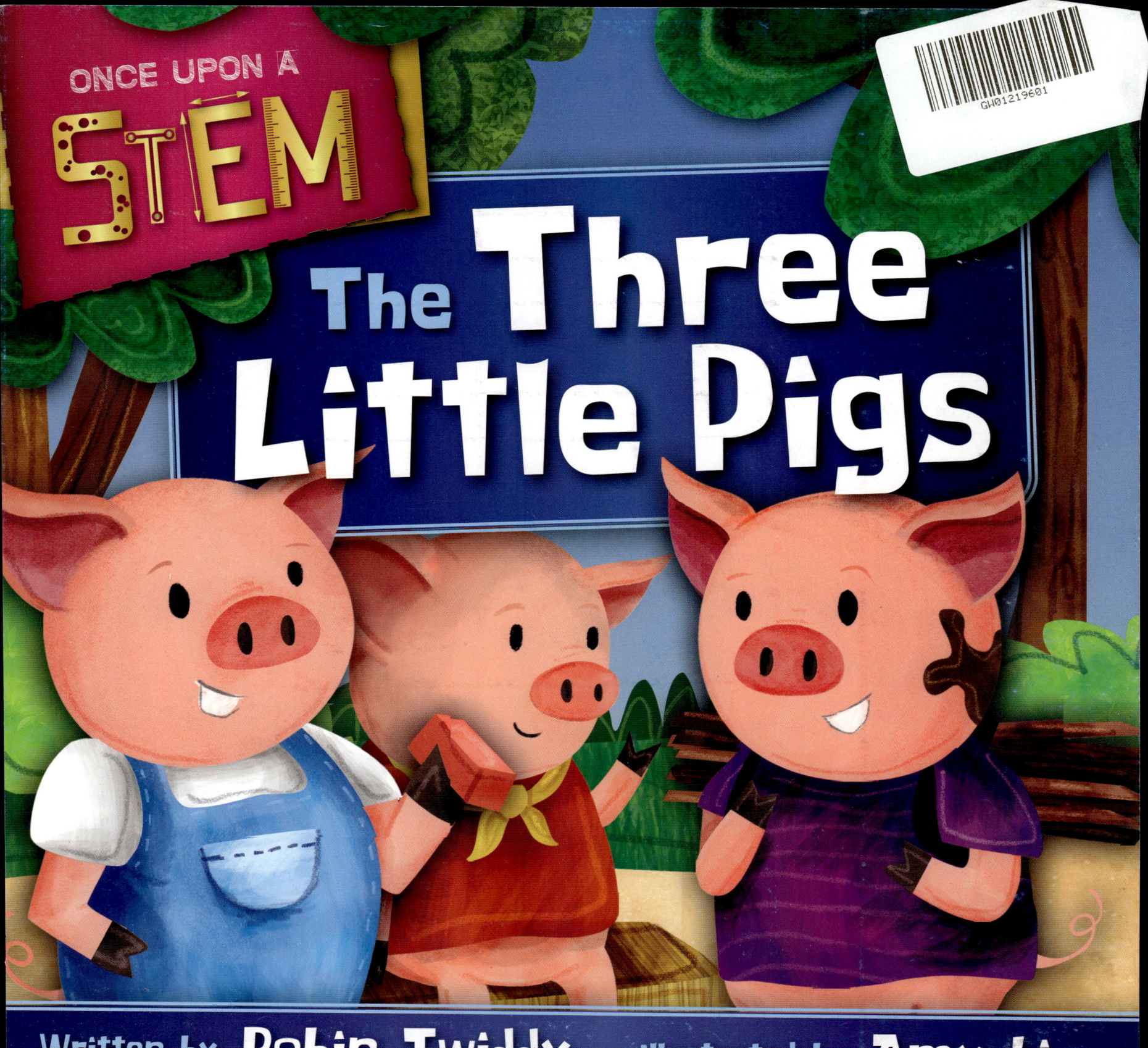

**BookLife**
PUBLISHING

©2021
BookLife Publishing Ltd.
King's Lynn
Norfolk PE30 4LS

ISBN: 978-1-83927-171-7

**Written by:**
Robin Twiddy

**Edited by:**
Madeline Tyler

**Designed by:**
Amy Li

A catalogue record for this book is available from the British Library.

All facts, statistics, web addresses and URLs in this book were verified as valid and accurate at time of writing. No responsibility for any changes to external websites or references can be accepted by either the author or publisher.

All rights reserved. Printed in Malaysia.

Words that look like this can be found in the glossary on page 24.

**Photo credits**

Recurring images (cover and internal) – artcreator (Professor), Yamabika, The_Pixel, MoonRock (paper textures), kotoffei, Venomous Vector, illustrator096 (decorative vectors), okawa somchai (leaf texture), Tanya Kalian (straw texture), p2–3 – Pretty Vectors, Tori20, P4–5 – wk1003mike, Alex Gontar, cluckva, p6–7 – art-sonik, p10–11 – Lightspring, p12–13 – wk1003mike, PCH.Vector, p14–15 – Lamcia, p16–17 – Lamcia, David Hagerman, p20–21 – wk1003mike, Angurt, LenaTru, Smach2003, gst, Mimadeo, p22–23 – Imichman, Rozova Anna, Pretty Vectors, Tori20. All images courtesy of Shutterstock.com. With thanks to Getty Images, Thinkstock Photo and iStockphoto.

Professor Everafter's lab, around bedtime...

"Welcome, I am Professor Everafter and I really like STEM subjects. These are science, technology, engineering and mathematics."

*The Three Little Pigs*

"Lately, I have been reading fairy tales. Some parts of these fairy tales would never work in real life. I've been trying to see if I can make them work using STEM! Here are my notes on The Three Little Pigs."

Once upon a STEM...

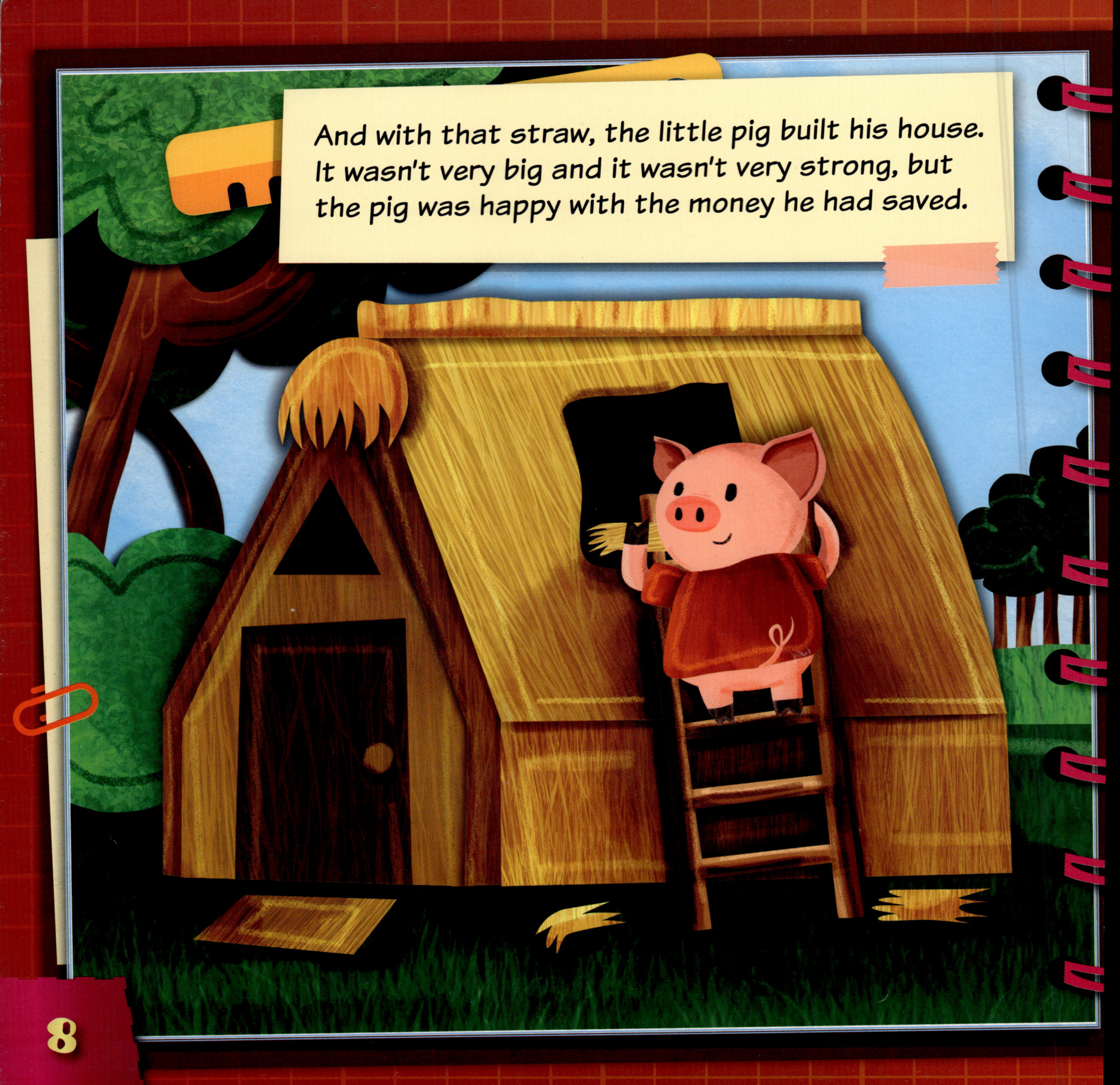
And with that straw, the little pig built his house. It wasn't very big and it wasn't very strong, but the pig was happy with the money he had saved.

The wolf could have caught that little piggy if he'd exercised more. Our lungs are important. They allow us to breathe and to take in <u>oxygen</u>. Our bodies need oxygen so they can work properly.

The more you exercise, the stronger your lungs will become, so you won't get out of breath so easily.

So, the little pig, feeling very good about saving some money, built his house of sticks. It was <u>sturdier</u> than his brother's house, but still cheap.

With this big fan — the kind used in wind tunnels and on movie sets — the Big Bad Wolf would be able to make a much stronger wind, and for much longer than he would be able to do with his mouth.

He also wouldn't be tired from all that blowing. He might even be able to catch the pig this time.

This time, the Big Bad Wolf wasn't going to let the little pig get away. He was ready to chase after him.

But this little pig had spent the money he had saved on an electric scooter. With a zoom, zoom, zoom, the little pig was gone.

The third little pig went to a <u>builders merchant</u> with his money and bought house bricks.

He also read a book on how to build houses. With the right tools and the right materials, this little piggy built a strong brick house.

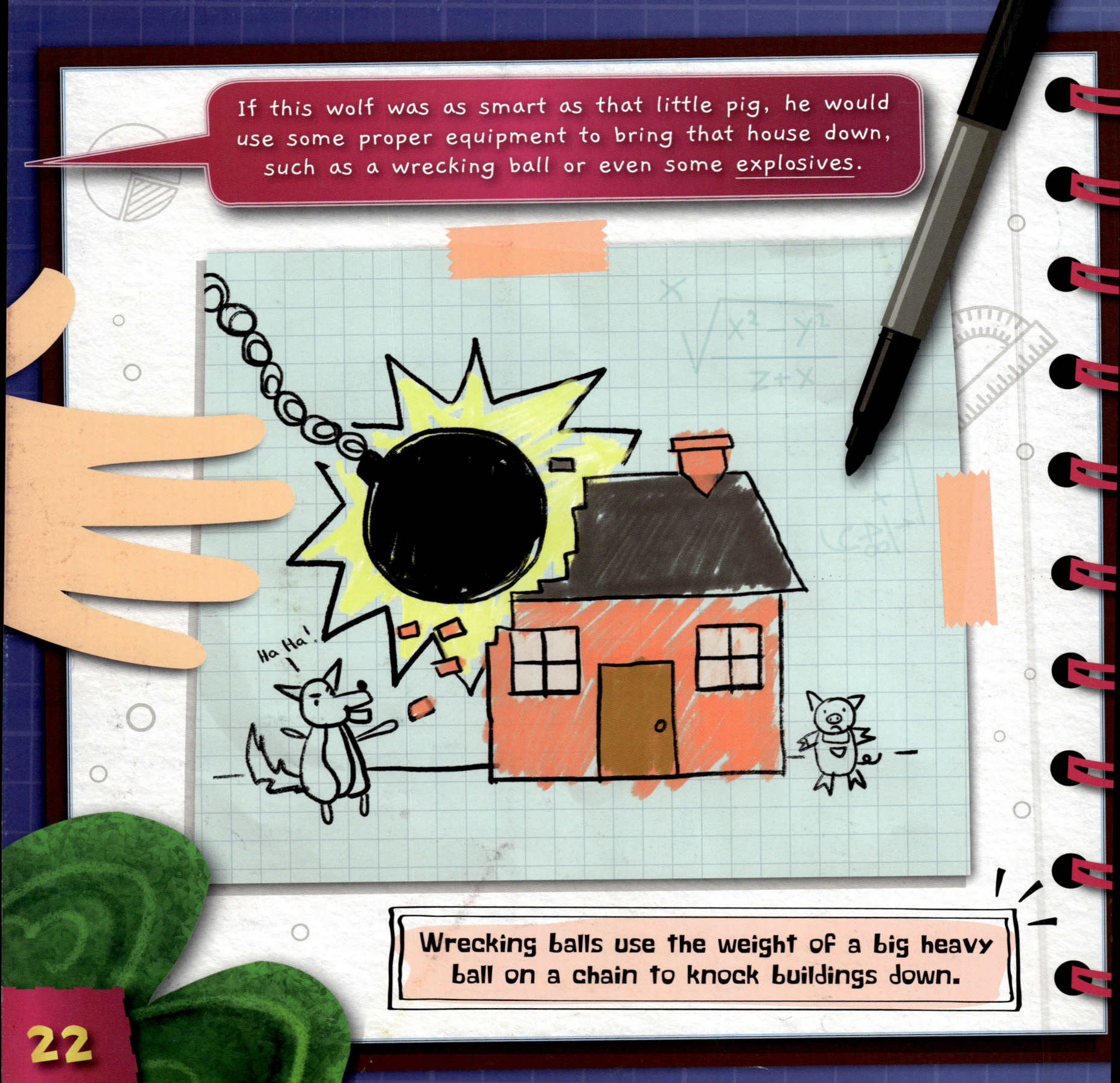

But, of course, the wolf didn't do that. He decided to climb down the chimney. He climbed straight into the little piggy's cooking pot and was made into a lovely wolf stew.

Well, that is one very silly wolf. If he had learned his STEM subjects, then he probably would have caught all three of those pigs.

# Glossary

| | |
|---|---|
| bales | large bundles of straw or hay that are packed together to be stored or transported |
| builders merchant | a place that sells building equipment and supplies |
| explosives | things that can explode and cause explosions, such as bombs |
| movie sets | areas where movies are filmed |
| oxygen | a natural gas that many living things need in order to survive |
| sturdier | stronger and less likely to fail |
| wind tunnels | places that use strong fans to test aircraft and cars against strong winds |

# Index

Big Bad Wolf 5, 9–10, 12–13, 16–19, 21–23
bricks 11, 20–21
engineering 3, 11, 20, 22
houses
- brick houses 20–22
- stick houses 15–17
- straw houses 8–11, 17

maths 3, 7, 14
science 3, 13
scooters 19
sticks 14–15, 17
straw 6–9, 11, 17
technology 3, 17–19, 21